AF470624

A
Woman's Own
World

Poignant and pertinent, sad or bitter-sweet, romantic or humorous, here is a stunning selection of the poems which appear weekly in *Woman's Own*.

A Woman's Own World

Janice James

ROBERT HALE · LONDON

This collection first published in Great Britain 1985

Robert Hale Limited
Clerkenwell House
Clerkenwell Green
London EC1R 0HT

Photoset in North Wales by
Derek Doyle & Associates, Mold, Clwyd.
Printed in Great Britain by
Photobooks (Bristol) Limited
and bound by WBC Bookbinders Limited.

British Library Cataloguing in Publication Data

James, Janice
    A Woman's Own world : the best of J.J.
    I. Title
    821'.914   PR6060.A457

ISBN 0-7090-2385-5

CONTENTS

LOVE LINES

TOGETHER

An ordinary man
Met an ordinary girl –
Extraordinary love story.

THE MATING REASON

Why is it men like women
Who adore them
While women chase after men
Who ignore them?

LOUISE

She's quite the prettiest child,
She's going to drive men wild
When she's older. And she's bright,
She does just everything right.
It might not be done to say
Your child scores in every way,
But I can, proudly, without hesitation …
For she's my god-daughter, no blood relation!

NOTHING'S PERFECT

She's marrying the man she loves,
To her life-long happiness he's vowed;
Pity she can't stand his mother –
Every silver lining has a cloud!

DUTY FREE?

We'd had such a fabulous holiday romance,
But, too soon, we had to part;
When the Customs asked me: "Anything to declare?"
I said, "I've a broken heart!"

DEAREST LOVE

He bought me an emerald ring,
And toasted me in champagne,
Asked me where we should honeymoon,
Italy, Germany, Spain?
Or would I prefer Brighton,
Or perhaps Paris instead?
I said that Bali beckoned –
"You're a dear, *dear* girl," he said!

PINK FOR A GIRL!

Don't notice I've got some grey hairs,
But mention I've had my hair done,
And don't remark I'm getting red,
Just say I've been kissed by the sun.
And don't say that I've put on weight,
An approach I find rather crass …
I don't want love to be blind, just
To see me through rose-tinted glass!

SLIM HOPE

I met this new man at a party,
"I hope I'll see more of you," he said,
But now that I'm on this strict diet –
I hope he'll see less of me instead!

LOVE FOR SALE

He swathed her in furs,
Took her to the best places,
Bought her a sports car,
Gave her diamond necklaces –
What could she want more?
She married the boy next door.
Isn't love funny?
You can't buy it with money.

NEVER TOO LATE

They said I'd be left on the shelf,
And that I shouldn't tarry,
Now, twelve years later, they're divorced …
And I'm about to marry.

SUPPOSING

Suppose a weeping willow laughed out loud,
And a silver lining hadn't a cloud;
Suppose Humpty Dumpty stayed on his wall
And little Tom Thumb grew up to be tall;
Suppose that runner beans started to walk –
Why not? Silent movies started to talk!
Suppose a busy Lizzie got lazy,
And suppose The Gang hadn't been Crazy;
Suppose we could recapture yesterday …
Could you love me again the same sweet way?

BROKEN PROMISE

You said we'd be together,
That our love would always last,
But now you've gone and left me –
Our future's become the past.

GIRL IN A MILLION

You said I was one in a million,
What I didn't know you meant then,
Was that I was one of the million
That you take out now and again!

BRIGHT BEGINNINGS

I watched him opening the door
As into the car you stepped,
And thought, early days, my dear …
You're obviously not married yet!

A QUESTION OF LOVE

So what was tomorrow like …
Was it good as you said it would be?
Yes, I'd really like to know –
Even though you spent it without me.

LONELY CROWD

Fifty people at the party,
I look around but, oh, my dear,
You've not arrived and so, for me,
It's just as though there's no one here.

UNLUCKY NUMBER

I counted the petals one by one,
Would my love last or would it be gone?
He loves me …
He loves me not …
He loves me …
He loves me not …
Does this mean our romance is over?
Why did I find this four-leaved clover!

MEMORIES

It was the *tenth* of May we met,
At that flat-warming given by Bill.
No, it wasn't Frank's. It was at Frank's
We quarrelled over that girl, Gill …
Yes, Gill, that dyed blonde with fat arms,
Don't pretend you've forgotten her name!
When you danced with her to *our* song … I
Must say your excuses were lame.
Dates, places, people I recall,
No recognition to your face bring,
While I've such a dreadful memory –
I never forget anything!

PARTINGS

You're back from abroad with lots of perfume,
You've brought me silver bracelets from Khartoum,
I've a drawer full of gifts from where you've been,
Souvenirs, momentoes of what you've seen.
You say (leaving),
"Of course we can have a video;
Arrange it, now I really must go."
I think (grieving):
Although you spend your money *on* me –
I'd prefer you to spend time *with* me.

OFFSIDE!

My love's so unromantic,
He really drives me frantic.
I give him a kiss
And he says, "What's this?
Why are you carrying on so –
We're not footballers, you know!"

ON THE SPOT

You went away so often
On your travels, my dear,
Absence made my heart fonder ...
Of someone who's right here!

GOODBYE TO THE DREAM

I will still walk in the fields of summer
And laugh and cry and sleep
As long day follows longer night.

And though my heart cannot believe it now
I know that life will still go on …

But there will be rain without rainbows,
Sundays without sun,
Love without love …
Me without you.

FOLLOWER OF FASHION

Dirndl skirts, cheesecloth shirts,
Baggy boots, trouser suits,
Embroidered braces, shoes with laces,
Knee-high socks, gingham smocks,
Riding macs, bell-bottom slacks,
Bishop sleeves, ethnic weaves,
Plus fours, pinafores,
Drainpipe pants, my giddy aunt's
Old lace shawl – I've tried them all …

But whatever I get that's in or new –
He still says "Why not wear the blue?"

AFTER SHAVE

My love has a beard
And I sometimes wonder
Is there a weak jaw or a double chin
Under?

HAIRY PROBLEM

My hair touched my waist,
Fashion said "out of date,"
So I had it cut short
And then met my fate.

He says he likes girls
With hair long, shiny, bright.
Please, how can I grow it —
By Saturday night?

PASSING STRANGERS

I wanted to say "You're looking great,"
And ask how the world was treating you.
I wanted to ask
If you remember
Irish sunsets,
French films,
Sunday afternoons looking at paintings,
Stopping for tea in little cafés.

I wanted to say "I like your tie,"
Find out if you still like autumn best.
I wanted to ask if you remember
Kew Gardens,
"Our" song,
Brighton on a day when the skies were green,
Long distance calls just to say "hello".

I wanted to say "I miss you" ...
But instead I just walked by.

ALL CHANGE

Flashing smile. Will I dance?
Here's to my holiday romance!
Swimming. Sunning. Kisses by moonlight.
Tearful goodbyes … And, of course, we'll write.
The months go by. The letters come late.
I try to remember – was he so great?

Where this year? Some place new for a start.
Change of place … change of heart.

SIGH

How can I describe
Feeling lonely …
In just two words –
If only.

LA DIFFÉRENCE

''Did anyone tell you,
You've lovely eyes?'' says he.
''I know he's thin and pimply
But he's intelligent,'' says she.

''Come on,'' he invites.
''Let's get out of here.''
''Tell me,'' she insists,
''What you're thinking, dear.''

''She's great. I fancy that,''
Leers our ageing hero.
His wife greets him after work –
''Now, how did your day go?''

The older one gets,
The more one finds –
Men want women's bodies –
Women, men's minds.

PRESENT DILEMMA

I had to buy *him* a present –
Didn't know which tie to choose,
So I brought him two – one bright yellow,
The other of many hues.
He said how much he liked them
And next time I saw him he wore
The yellow one; it looked quite nice
But now I'm really not sure.
I mean, can anyone tell me why
He didn't wear the other tie?

TRUE LOVE

You're fat and bald and rather short,
A rabbit on the tennis court.
You're not the man to stand out in a crowd
And your suits are really rather loud.
You'll never be rich, that's perfectly plain
As the nose on your face … But then, again,
I like your smile, your voice – the way you
mop up my tears …
Yes, I think I'd like you around for
the next fifty years.

GONE, BUT ...

Please don't talk about him
Now he's gone.
If you do –
I won't be able to carry on.

LONESOME TRAVELLER

The South of France
Doesn't stand a chance.
I've been to Jahore –
It's a bore.
Even Rome in the sun
Is no fun.
You can keep Biarritz, New York and Corfu,
Los Angeles, Madrid and London, too.

The world's just a sphere ...
When you're not here.

STAYING POWER

I prefer trees to flowers;
Trees start from small beginnings
And grow a little more each year –
Like love.

I prefer trees to flowers;
Flowers grow, bloom and dazzle,
Then suddenly fade and die –
Like love.

BREAKING UP

No, please don't stay,
Don't try to be kind,
If you don't want me,
Leave me behind.
Go away now,
Don't ever pretend.
Goodbye is kinder,
You'll find in the end.

STAR-CROSSED LOVERS

He's tall, dark and handsome,
Brave, witty, a great dancer,
But how can I marry him?
He's Capricorn – I'm Cancer!

APPEARANCES

Here I am wearing my false eyelashes
And smiling my false smile,
Saying the things I think you want to hear,
Wondering all the while –
Would you like the *real* me?

BITTER SWEET

Memories are cruel,
Memories are kind,
But I'm so grateful
You left them behind.

MAN-SHOT

They've put men in space,
Men on the moon,
Could they put a man
In my life – soon?

WARNING SIGNS

You say you don't find her very pretty,
Remark when she's older how fat she'll get,
And you say she's more witless than witty –
So that, dear, is why I know she's a threat!

MADE FOR EACH OTHER

I love you, hate you,
Isn't it clear
There's no one but you
For me, my dear ...?

END OF A PERFECT EVENING

I'd such a marvellous evening,
I knew I had impressed,
So why is it I'm now back home
And feeling so depressed?
I thought that I was in heaven,
Not on this earth beneath,
But I've just looked in the mirror –
There's lipstick on my teeth!

ONCE UPON A TIME

Do I remember the scent of roses,
The way the sun always seemed to shine?
Do I still remember that small café
Where you swore you would always be mine?
Do I recall that wishing well in Spain,
The wines we have drunk, the songs we have sung …
Oh, and do I remember that day when …?
Of course I don't, darling – I'm far too young!

FOOD FOR
THOUGHT

HOME COOKING

He said he thought I should learn to cook,
He even went out and bought me a book.
I said I'd take some lessons, to please,
Then, when I served him bread and cheese,
He asked me if this were Cordon Bleu –
I said: "I've been on a sandwich course, sir!"

ENOUGH SAID

You may eat what you like, but sparingly,
This diet's praises I do not sing,
All I can say while my mouth waters ...
You can have too little of a good thing!

COLD COMFORT

Ten pounds of plums,
Six dozen buns,
Two flanks of sheep,
A veritable heap
Of peas and beans
And some terrines.
Two dozen quiches,
Jellied peach;
Still there are spaces –
Okay – pastry cases.
Half a pig –
Oh, lord, it's big …

As I slave away,
It seems to me,
I don't own my freezer –
My freezer owns me!

TEMPTATION

Oh, why did I do it
When so much was at stake …
Ruining my diet
For a chocolate milk shake!

COOK WITHOUT A CAUSE

I've got masses of cookery books,
Done a course at Cordon Bleu,
My boeuf en croûte is sensational –
You should taste my pot-au-feu.
My family's unappreciative,
They always ask for the same:
Eggs, sausages, beans, bacon and chips –
Isn't it a frying shame!

CAN COOK, CAN'T COOK

Now, please, do not grumble
At my apple crumble;
Yes, there's less in the pie
Than at first meets the eye.
I know I've made a hash
Of the carrots and mash,
But don't get in a stew
Let me explain to you:
You say I can't cook, I can –
I can, but the cans can't!
This meal's not Cordon Bleu,
The reason is, dear sir,
That the cans are not able
To live up to their label!

UNWELCOME INVITATION

One thing that has always worried me,
I wonder if you have the answer? Pray,
When cannibals have guests for dinner –
Do they mean literally what they say?

MATHEMATICAL WIZARD

Lunching with my friend Jill
Really isn't a treat,
She can't add two and two
But when we start to eat
She looks at my plate and,
With the greatest of ease,
Tells me it adds up to
A thousand calories!

KITCHEN HITCH

It's no use crying over spilt milk?
That's all very well to say,
But the shops are closed, my guests are here,
And I planned to serve soufflé!

GOURMET DINNER

What shall we have for dinner?
I go through my repertoire:
Would you like duck à l'orange,
Or steak with pâté de foie?
My husband shows no interest,
But I plough on: Fish? Pot roast?
"Just use your loaf", he says, bored ...
So I gave him beans on toast!

P.S. He loved it!

COOKERY HINT

No offence intended,
And I hope none you'll take,
But I really can't stand the thought of
Pies like your mother used to make!

SOUR APPLES

I must say I find it hard to believe
That Adam really was tempted by Eve
With an apple. I cannot see at all
How that boring fruit could bring his downfall.
No! 'Twas a potato, not an apple,
With which Adam's conscience had to grapple,
And the moment when he started to slip
Was when Eve offered him a golden chip!

FOOD 'N' WINE

They say use cheap wine when you're cooking,
A thought that's not very merry,
When I'm slaving over a hot stove –
I drink the very best sherry!

HERE'S HEALTH!

Now is the run-up to bikini time,
And that means getting into trim,
So decided to go on a diet,
As well as work out at the gym.
I went off to the local health food shop,
In this attempt to save myself,
But the notice on the door put me off:
"We're closed – owing to staff ill-health"!

BEAUTY BAR

Think of your skin
Before you drink gin.
Beer? –
No fear.
Vodka, rum, even sherry
Won't make your beautician
Very merry.
No, not brandy,
It might be handy
For Cordon Bleu cooks
But for your looks
It's as risky
As whisky.
For your face
You ought'a
Concentrate
On water.
P.S. I finished the rhyme
Before they called "time".

COOKS' TOUR

Spaghetti in Rome with
Chianti and fresh rolls.
On a small Greek island,
Fish soup in steaming bowls.

German sausage, French bread,
Dutch herrings, Irish stew;
Paella in Palma,
Moussaka on Corfu.

Portugal's fresh sardines,
Swiss chocolate with cream,
Turkish delight, kebabs,
Are foods of which to dream.

In a small inn in France,
Steak au poivre (with chips),
Travel broadens the mind? –
Well, it broadens the hips!

ABSENT FRIENDS

An apple a day
Keeps the doctor away …
An onion a day
Keeps the whole world at bay!

AGEING WELL

Sometimes I think that, nowadays,
When youth is all the rage,
It must be nice to be brandy –
And just improve with age!

FOOD FOR THOUGHT

You are a man after my own heart,
A man who likes beef, Yorkshire, fruit tart.
When you asked me to dinner,
I thought I was a winner …
But what did I gain?
The thought gives me pain …
For I have gained a whole stone,
Now, do please leave me alone,
Why we can't go on meeting like this,
Is: because I can't go on eating like this!

DARK THOUGHT!

Oh, how I long for somebody to state,
"You're the shadow of your former self";
After years of eating carbohydrate,
I'm the *substance* of my former self!

LOVING CUP

Drink to me only with thine eyes —
For drunken men I do despise!

DATE LINES

REMEMBRANCE DAY

You see them now,
Old people, afraid to walk the street,
Managing on small means,
Unable to afford meat or heat.

Think of them then,
Young people, fighting for this nation,
Leaving their homes, jobs, loves,
To give their youth, dreams, dedication.

But for them we'd not be here,
Yet we let them live in fear
And poverty. Heroes,
Who we treat like zeroes.

Let us remember them today …
And not forget them tomorrow.

EACH DAY AS IT COMES

Oh, why do you spend *these* good times,
Worrying that they won't last,
And regretting all *those* good times,
Wishing that they weren't past?
Enjoying the moment makes sense,
Life should be lived in the present tense.

DAY IN, DAY OUT

You know they say don't worry,
For tomorrow is another day?
Well, that's what's worrying me –
Suppose tomorrow's just like today!

SEASONS

In Spring the world goes out in pairs,
That's why I don't like Spring.

I prefer Autumn
When loves that bloomed with summer, die –

And Winter waits with its warm darkness
To hide my loneliness.

WIMBLEDON FORTNIGHT

I shop, cook, wash, iron, clean,
For fifty weeks of the year,
But now, my dear family,
I'd like to make it clear:
The next two weeks are all mine,
(Yes, there's a note of menace),
Don't bother me, don't disturb –
Mother is watching tennis!

HAPPY CHRISTMAS!

My daughter can't be home for Christmas
But she's sent me a really nice shawl,
And my son's going to his in-laws,
He can't get out of it for they all
Are expected. Still, they'll try to phone
Me on Boxing Day and hope I like
Their crystal glasses, and my grandson
Is so very thrilled with his new bike.
The neighbours are going away. They
Brought me round a bottle of sherry,
My nephew has sent me a hamper,
Wishing me a Christmas that's merry.

Yes, everybody's bought me something …
Nobody's given me anything.

MY GUY

Please don't forget the Fifth of November,
It's our anniversary – remember!

HELPMATE

\'ll cut down on drink, cut out smoking,
Lose half a stone, no, I'm not joking,
I'll get up early, make morning tea,
No one will recognise this new me.
My partner I'll help, appreciate,
From now on, I'll never be home late …
There you are, darling, you've no more to do –
I've made New Year resolutions for *you*!

CHRISTMAS NEVER GOES!

Christmas comes but once a year?
Don't try to fool me, my dear …
It starts around the middle of October
And stays at least two months before it's over!

SEASON'S GREETINGS

To old friends and new friends,
And the people next door,
Everyone at the office,
And relatives galore,
The milkman, the grocer,
The doctor and (I groan)
To my bank manager
To melt his heart of stone.
My card list is complete,
There, I've finished the lot …
Why's the first card I get
From someone I forgot!

A YEAR OF VERSES

January
Winter sales, sudden gales,
Beastly chills, heating bills,
Snowball fights, cosy nights,
Scarlet-nosed, warmly-hosed,
Greet New Year with a cheer.

February
No more sun, days soon done,
Pancakes tossed, rain and frost,
Don't decline, Valentine!
Yes, snowdrops … but cough drops,
Lowest ebb … forget Feb!

March
First bluebells, primrose dells,
Daffodils, nature thrills,
Pale gold sun, winter's done,
Without words, early birds
Praises sing to fair Spring.

April
April's here! Poets cheer,
Rush to praise limpid days,
Showers? So … Rainbows grow
And jonquils. Brings tax bills,
But the while, daisies smile.

May
Lambs gambol, bushes bramble,
Cream teas, strawberries,
Peaches, topless beaches,
Just some gloom, exams loom –
But May, merry? – Very!

June
Green-clad trees, bumble bees,
Gold-flecked land, scorching sand,
Azure skies, seagulls' cries,
Garden teas, white-crowned seas,
Days so long – Summer's song.

July
School reports, packed resorts,
Home from school, children rule,
Picnic days, mothers dazed,
Swithin's Day – rain stops play –
Sweet July flashes by.

August
Park brass bands, foreign lands,
Coconut shies, wasps, flies,
Salad teas, sunburnt knees,
Day-tripping, tops whipping,
August is family bliss.

September
Leaf-strewn dells, birds' farewells,
Purple haze, fruity days,
Joy! Behold, Nature's gold,
Rich, ripe corn, misty morn,
Grateful come, harvest home.

October
Schools reprise, coloured trees,
Conker wars, great outdoors,
Gather logs, 'bye hedgehogs,
Final scene, Hallowe'en,
Soon over, October.

November
Naked trees, rivers freeze,
Buttered toast, chestnuts roast,
Bonfire Night, wrap up tight,
Trains delay. Poppy Day,
Remember ... November.

December
Bells jingle, hands tingle,
Robin bright, a brave sight,
People hurry, snowflakes scurry,
Carols sing, Christ is King.
Air ice-clear, Winter's here.

FAMILY LIFE

SCENT OF HAPPINESS

Father's deep in the paper,
Daughter shiny morning clean,
Son's still doing his homework –
Warm family breakfast scene.
Baby gurgles happily,
This is the time I love most,
All of us close together –
And the smell of burning toast!

STARRING ROLE

I'm a mother, a daughter, a secretary, a wife –
What am I doing with my life?
The scenes are banal, the plot is hoary –
Why can't I be the star of my own life story?

LET'S FORGET OUR DIFFERENCES

If we don't stop this
Battle of the sexes,
You'll find we'll end up
As each other's ex-es.

MATERNAL FEELINGS

When I was twenty
I said:
When I have children,
They'll be smart, pretty,
Be good at small talk,
Brilliant, witty,
Play the piano,
Dance, swim, ski, ride, and
Sail through their exams,
Be much in demand ...

Now I am thirty,
I say:
If I have children,
I've no big plans,
They needn't go far,
And I will love them —
Just as they are.

TO A BABY

Because you cannot talk,
I think you do not understand.
But already
You know what love is.
You see it in my eyes.

Because you cannot walk,
I think you are helpless.
But already
You know power.
You cry and I come running.

Love and power –
Already you know
What life is all about.

SOCIAL WHIRL

We're much in demand in society,
If a new club opens, we're there.
For parties, we invite eighty close friends,
We know who's who, what's what and where's where.

Each weekend you'll find us in the country,
Or, if in town, at some trendy pub,
And no first night is complete without us,
Of all social events, we're the hub.

We go everywhere – we'll even visit his mother,
Anything, rather than be alone with each other.

COLOUR BLIND

Happy baby,
Smile so bright,
Father is black,
Mother is white.

What colour's the child
Of the couple above?

The colour of love.

MY FAMOUS SON

I tell my son he should study law
But he doesn't react at all.
So how about medicine, I ask myself ...
Oh, but no, he'd be always on call.

Well, how about acting – another Finney?
He could be a great superstar.
But he says nothing – just mumbles away.
Whatever he does – he'll go far.

But I'd like the law. I can see him now
So handsome in silk robes and wig –
A judge. Already? Now, steady on,
There's a long way to go. Still, think big!

I plan for his future, say what I think
But it all seems to leave him cold.
Ah, well, one day he'll decide for himself ...
After all, he's just six months old.

SECOND HONEYMOON

After twelve years of marriage,
A holiday together, alone,
It will be so romantic
But we must remember to take home
Presents for the family ...
I think a train set for our son,
He said he'd behave himself
And do his homework while we are gone.
For our daughter a dressed doll –
She's got such a lovely collection,
For dad, cigars, and for mum,
The sweetest chocolate confection ...
And for my mother-in-law
Some cheese, all smelly and runny –

How did we spend our weekend?
Right! You guessed it – we spent our money!

COST OF LIVING

Two can live as cheaply as one –
A saying I find a vexation.
More like one can live as cheaply as two –
Allowing for inflation.

DEJA VU

I watch you leaving for the dance,
So pretty on your first real date ...
Trying to look calm, sure of yourself
(You were so worried he'd be late).

You introduced him to dad and me –
You'd asked me to wear my green dress
And you'd even lent me your lipstick
(You were so eager to impress) ...

So I forgave the implied insult
I know so well you didn't mean ...
I remember many years ago
And a very similar scene ...

Am I really old enough to have
A daughter with the looks I had –
And that gangling youth in the doorway –
Does he really look like your dad?

AN IDEAL HUSBAND

What a considerate man,
So attentive to his wife,
Nothing is too good for her,
To her every judgement he'll defer.
Thoughtful, gentle, ever present –
These days I find it very pleasant.
So what mad devil makes me say –
He'd drive *me* nuts in half a day!

COMPETITION

Oh, no, here it comes again,
The Miss World competition;
Getting you to look at me
Is now my sole ambition …
But "Miss Ireland," you drool,
Or "Miss Sweden – she's so cool."
Miss Ghana's great, so's Peru,
Miss England's eyes are so blue!
It's wow "Miss This" or "Miss That,"
So I'm telling where it's at …
Walking out the door, I say:
"Maybe you'll 'Miss Me' someday!"

WHOSE BABY?

You boast that your daughter is lovely,
While mine is a lazy slut,
And your son's a computer wizard,
And mine should get his hair cut.
Your girl's a paragon of virtue,
My daughter's always home late,
Your son's good at sport, mine drinks too much,
These comparisons I hate.
When they're doing well, our children you claim –
Let them do badly … *my* kids are to blame!

MIXED FEELINGS

"I'd like to go to Eton," said I.
"But that's a boys' school," was dad's reply.
Exactly!

YOUTH CULT

My husband thinks you can stay young forever,
Like Dorian Gray … and to this end he does
endeavour
To eat and drink the minimum,
And exercise the maximum –
Not only is he a keep-fit fanatic,
He keeps a photo of himself, when young,
in the attic!

COUP DE GRÂCE

We've sown and watered, fertilised,
But we're feeling demoralised –
We must admit, alack, alas,
Our lawn just doesn't grow like grass!

FREE EXCHANGE

My son is very cheeky,
But witty, I can't deny,
I said I'd give him a piece of my mind –
''Gee, mum, thanks for *nothing*!'' was his reply.

DECEPTION

How can it all have ended like this?
How could I have not understood
It would all turn out for the bad –
I thought we were marrying for good!

THE NAME'S RIGHT!

New uniform needed,
He's grown another size,
School trip in the offing,
"Please may I go?" he cries.
It's money for this,
It's money for that ...
Now he'd like a new bike,
Afford it if we will –
No wonder we call him
Our boy, *Bill*!

FAMILY GATHERING

We're having a family picnic
On this lovely summer's day,
The food is good, the drink is better,
And nobody's stayed away.
There are more than two hundred of us –
You're evincing some surprise? –
Well, there's me and he and four children ...
The ants, the wasps and the flies!

BREAKFAST BLUES

"I don't feel well, I can't go to school,"
My son moans, while dad comes down to say:
"*Your* daughter's still in the bathroom
And you know I've a big day today."
The tea gets cold as tempers get hot,
The baby is sick and starts to cry,
The post is all bills, the toast is burnt,
Now can anyone please tell me why
Other families rise and shine,
But as for mine, they rise and whine?

TIME DIFFERENCE

Why, darling, it is nice to hear from you,
Of course I'm alone, why shouldn't we talk?
What do you mean, you worried about me –
What was I doing? I went for a walk ...
Yes, a walk. Just to see the city lights,
No, I'm not lying, please, dearest, don't *squawk* –
Look, it might be three in the morning there,
But it's only ten o'clock in New York!

GREEN EYES

My husband says I'm jealous,
That this time I've gone too far –
Just because I looked in his diary,
And then asked him who May and June are!

THAT'S MARRIAGE!

The car is due for a service,
The washing machine's on the blink,
And all the children need new shoes –
It's enough to drive you to drink.
Oh, yes, the kitchen needs painting,
And the bathroom and garden shed,
Oh, was it only yesterday
That we were painting the town red!

CLEVER BOY!

He gave me a pottery ashtray,
Though I don't smoke, it filled me with glee,
For my son made it for me himself.
It cost nothing? – It's priceless to me.

HOBBY HORSES

I took up classes in art,
For a while I painted madly,
Grew bored, tried bridge, golf, Spanish,
Then turned my back on them gladly.
I think I might learn guitar,
"What next?" asks my husband sadly,
But if a thing's worth doing …
It's even worth doing badly.

'PHONE MOAN

Whoever said that talk is cheap,
Didn't have teenage kids, that's clear,
For when I look at my 'phone bills,
I know that talk is very dear!

HOLIDAY HAVOC

Oh, how I dreamed of a castle in Spain,
And my husband took the hint,
Bought a time-share ... a week each November
(He forgot to read the small print!)

FIRST DAY

I'd looked forward to this day when
I'd be able to be *me* again,
Do all the things I planned I'd do,
Not always be thinking about you ...
But the day's dragged; I'm so glad you're here –
Home from your first day at school, my dear!

SOUNDING OFF

I love you, you love me,
What could I ask for more?
Only some genius
With a cure for your snore!

IDENTITY CRISIS

Would you miss me?
Or would you just notice you have no clean socks,
Dinner isn't on the table
And no one's wound up the clocks?
Would you miss me ...
Or groan I hadn't made the bed,
Make yourself a sandwich and think that the room
Needs dusting and the cat's not fed?
What am I to you?
The woman who cares for your needs,
Or the woman you care about?
Would you miss me ...
Me?

NAVY BLUES

All the nice girls love a sailor,
If they could only have their pick?
Does this mean I'm not a nice girl –
My husband's always so sea-sick!

EAR, EAR!

Searched everywhere for my ear-ring,
Feared that forever it was gone,
But now, at last, I have found it –
In the ear of my teenage son!

SCATTERBRAIN

You complain I'm very scatty,
And your sarcasm really chills,
But why not specify light bulbs –
Then I'd not have bought daffodils!

WALK-OUT

You say you're walking out on me,
Well, you won't get very far ...
Yes, you're definitely *walking* out,
For you're not taking the car!

A WOMAN'S WORK

Wake the family, make the breakfast, first of
three meals of the day,
Make the school run, stack the dishes, do the
washing – whites look grey!
Grab a sandwich, clean the windows, join a queue
for week's shopping,
Do ironing and the mending, help with homework –
eyelids dropping ...

A woman's work is never done

To park with baby, meet other mothers; we pass
the time of day,
Coffee morning, call at library, go to daughter's
first school play,
Make fudge with children, watch telly, husband brings
me home some flowers,
My steak pie's praised (so's apple crumble), baby
sleeps eight hours ...

A woman's work is often fun.

ROLE REVERSAL

Ignore what people say,
We're living life our way,
And what does it matter,
As long as *we're* happy
That I'm changing a tyre
While you change a nappy?

THAT'S ENTERTAINMENT!

The Smiths have just called to cancel,
And the cleaners haven't sent back my dress,
The joint looks tough as an old boot,
The kids have left the bathroom in a mess.
The dog's been sick on the carpet,
Was anyone ever in such a plight?
No, don't try to reassure me –
I *know* it will be all wrong on the night!

SOUNDPROOF

If only once you listened to me,
Instead of saying, ''Yes, of course, dear,''
I'd ask all my friends to vote for you –
As The Man of the Ear!

TOO QUIET FOR COMFORT?

Oh bliss! Oh joy! the children asleep,
At the end of a long, long day.
Pour me a drink, dear, it's so nice
To relax. Shall we watch the play?
The children went off straight away,
And they usually take so long,
Oh bliss! Oh joy! Oh dear! Oh me! …
Do you think something could be wrong?

MODEL WIFE

The fridge needs defrosting,
The telly's on the blink,
I've run out of polish,
Something's blocked up the sink.
My plants are all wilting,
My "cuisine's" not "nouvelle",
I've the Good Housekeeping
Seal of Disapproval!

DRESSED TO KILL

Two sweaters,
Two skirts,
Hat, shoes, gloves,
Three shirts.
Planning my wardrobe?
Alas, no fear.
My daughter's starting
Her new school year!

CHILD'S PLAY

The instructions on electronic toys
Really do sort out the men from the boys.
My husband bought our son the latest "thing",
He was finally reduced to saying:
"Yes, it *is* simple, that I do admit –
So simple *only* a child could work it!"

PRESENT PROBLEMS

He gave me a black lace negligée,
And I gave him a pair of slippers,
He gave me a diaphanous blouse,
And I gave him a box of kippers,
He gave me a gold-plated toothpick,
And I gave him a waterproof mac.
He's really keen on his presents …
Tomorrow, I'm taking mine back!

BEAR UP!

I promise I won't hurt him, though it's
Tough on the patient, I fear.
I'll put in the stitches just like this,
No, please, don't panic, my dear.
There, see what a lovely job I've made ...
Of sewing back Teddy's ear!

THIS IS MY LIFE!

Wash the dishes first, or make the beds,
Or do the garden – all those dead heads,
Should those curtains go to the laundry? ...
They're so dirty – quite extraordinary;
There's dry rot, rising damp, rusting –
Can't I settle for some light dusting?
Or do aerobics, work up a sweat?
Take the cat to the vet (come here, pet!) ...
Isn't life fun? My heart rejoices ...
To know I've got so many choices!

ALL IN THE SAME BOAT

Our friends are persuading us not to part,
They ask what we'll do without each other,
Think of the house and think of the children,
What on earth will you say to his mother?
We appreciate what they are saying
But we've arrived at this sad conclusion,
They want us together, just as they are,
With their failures, deceits, disillusion.

HOME COMFORTS

Five hours' delay on the outward flight.
Two bottles of lotion – mosquitoes bite!
Packed beaches. Sunburn. Undercooked meat.
Tea that tastes funny. And walk-weary feet.
Hidden expenses that make you groan …
Isn't it nice to be staying at home!

HINDSIGHT

What a wonderful holiday we had,
So many places to which we've been,
Now let's look at all those photos we took –
And see what we're supposed to have seen!

TOGETHERNESS

How will it look?
What will *they* say?
What does it matter if
We're living life *our* way?

TAKE IT FROM ME

Now, promise, you won't be too late,
Are you sure you'll get home all right?
And watch how much they give you to drink,
Isn't that skirt a little bit tight?
Let me help you with your eye-shadow,
The way you apply it is crummy,
Now do have a very nice time –
But, please, do be careful, mummy!

GROUNDS FOR DIVORCE

You don't notice I've had my hair done,
Or that I've lost several pounds,
And, don't you see, this is a new dress,
I really think I've got grounds
For divorce for you never notice …
That's why I find it shocking,
Even though I'm wearing a long skirt –
You spot the hole in my stocking!

CLEVER LADY

What's his is ours,
But as for mine –
It's in a bank
In Liechtenstein!

BED-TIME STORY

Double beds are so over-rated,
Why sleep in one just because we're mated?
I hog the blankets, sometimes you snore,
So we find we're making not love – but war!
I can't sleep with you – you toss and turn,
So why don't we a simple lesson learn:
When one sleeps sound and the other less –
Single beds make for double happiness!

FOOD FOR THOUGHT

I'll just finish this buttered toast
The children didn't eat.
And I can put that dish away
If I eat this last sweet.
I spoon up the cold potato
Thinking that a housewife
Has a very difficult choice
To make about her life:
It's
What a waste!
Or
What a waist!

IS THERE LIFE AFTER MARRIAGE?

Enjoy yourself before
You settle down, they said –
But we got married and
Enjoy ourselves instead.

CONTRASTS

I look at my friend,
She's had lovers galore,
She's travelled the world
But she always craves more.

She laughs at me for
I married at eighteen,
(I'd met so few men,
So few places I'd seen).

I sometimes envy
All the things she has done.
Have I missed out on
Life? Have I missed the fun?

But then, my husband,
With love I look at you,
And know it's nice when
Your past's your future too.

PILLOW TALK

Now don't blame our friends
When you ask me why I weep.
No one told me a thing –
You just talk in your sleep!

WHY?

This is where it all finishes,
Where our marriage ends,
The reason is very simple –
We just *weren't* good friends.

ILLICIT PLEASURES

Remember we cuddled
In the backs of parked cars,
At parties, at bus-stops,
And in dimly-lit bars?
Longing for privacy
But always frustrated
(When our parents went out,
How we were elated!)

And here we are married
In this big double bed,
Ignoring each other –
Watching telly instead!

SHARING

So now we're leaving,
Finished with grieving.
No more caring,
Time for sharing
Out our home sweet home.

You take the settee,
The silver's for me;
Take that carpet,
I don't like it –
Leave me the armchair.

Whatever we've got,
We must halve the lot –
You this, me that,
But there's our cat …
Did you think of that?

THE PERFECT WIFE

Oh, must you leave the tap dripping?
Would you kindly move those books ...
There's lots to do in the garden ...
Will you put up some kitchen hooks?

Don't walk mud all over the place,
I've just cleaned the house, can't you see?
I don't know why I married you ...
What do you mean? – *You're* leaving *me*!

SECOND TIME AROUND

My children are ashamed of me,
They say my dresses are cut too low,
They object to the way I dance –
(For I'd rather rock than dance a ''slow'').
They say my make-up's too heavy,
And my language isn't always nice ...
I ignore them, do my own thing,
For, after all, you're only young – twice!

POLES APART?

She's so quiet, he holds forth,
She likes the sun, he heads North;
She's always early, he late,
Yet today they celebrate
Their tenth anniversary.
What's their secret? Seems to be ...
Incompatability!

PICK-ME-UP

In life's rich tapestry,
There are so many hitches,
I'm glad you're always there
To pick up my dropped stitches.

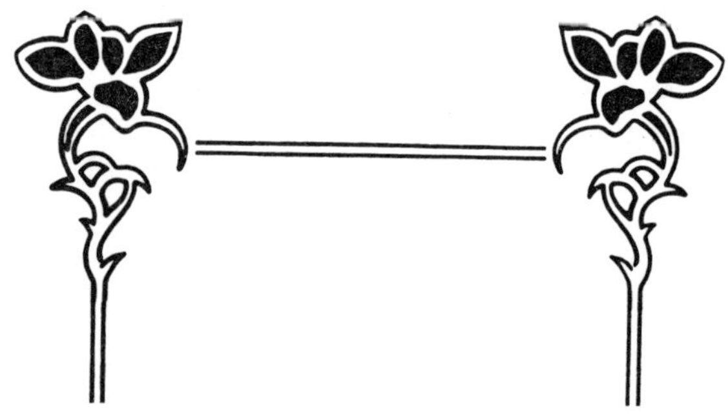

LAUGH LINES

THINK BIG!

A penny for my thoughts,
Is that what you offer me?
Just make that fifty pence –
It's inflation, don't you see!

SOUNDING BRASS

Money talks, they say
And I'd so like to hear it.
Not a chance, I fear –
I never do get near it!

TIME GOES BY SO SLOWLY

When I was a child,
There were certain actresses,
Lovely, talented,
I followed their successes …
And now I'm grown up
And I sometimes wonder how
They're younger than me
When I read about them now!

HOSTESS WITH THE LEASTEST

That's fascinating – oh, excuse me,
Some other guests have arrived, you see …
I'd really like to know what you think,
But I must get Joan another drink …
Introduce yourselves – I'll check the food,
I hope you don't think I'm very rude,
But when I'm entertaining, dear me,
I'm not entertaining company!

THE BOTTOM LINE

Though she wears expensive designer pants,
Her hips still look much bigger than her friend's,
And she only bought off-the-peg denims ...
Sadly, though we may do our bumps and bends,
It's the genes,
Not the jeans,
That shape our ends!

JET SET

Diamonds and emeralds, silks and furs,
Twin private planes labelled "his" and "hers".
Don't you think we should have a third home?
Where it's at — New York, Paris or Rome?
Where's the champagne, the party, what gives? ...
Oh, how the other half (per cent!) lives!

ADULT ENTERTAINMENT

The playground is deserted,
The children all at school,
So nobody will notice …
Come on, let's play the fool!
It seems only yesterday,
We, too, would swing and slide,
Quick, jump on the roundabout,
And let's enjoy the ride!

DISTRESSED TRESSES

Now that the man in my life has gone,
I don't think I can carry on.
He says he's going to live in Spain,
How can I face the world again?
What on earth am I going to do?
Who can I turn to? I'm so blue …
But why on earth should I get a divorce? –
It's my hairdresser who's leaving, of course!

CAR SICK

Check mirror – goodness, I look wan!
Yes, I am listening … I'll switch on.
Clutch, accelerator, first gear –
Now, what's that funny noise I hear?
The hand brake's off … Oh, it needs choke?
Drat! Broken my nail! It's no joke …
These driving lessons, I declare,
Will surely drive me to despair!

ONLY THE GOOD DIE …!

She was an example to us all!
He was a citizen so fearless;
This one never thought an evil thought,
Another man's described as peerless …
The cemetery is filled with grave errors
of judgement!

DIAMOND LIL

My best friend has just got engaged,
Oh, how she does crow and purr,
It's a vulgarly large diamond,
So large, I'm sure you'll concur:
That she isn't wearing the ring –
It's the ring that's wearing her!

LITTLE ENGLANDER

I've tried to learn Spanish to no avail,
At languages I always fail.
Italian? German? French? No point – merci!
You see, it's all just Greek to me.

POSITIVE THINKING

If I skip a meal I feel I should lose
half a stone,
If my bank manager smiles I'm sure I'll get
that loan,
I expect a man to propose after I've been
kissed –
Guess I'm the eternal optimist!

UNWILLINGLY TO SCHOOL

The history teacher hates me,
She gives me extra work,
And I hate games practice,
The sports captain says I shirk.
I'm the school bully's victim,
We're constantly in strife ...
Please don't let these be the
Happiest days of my life!

COMMON OR GARDEN? VERY ...!

I wanted to study bird life,
Attract different species to my garden,
So I took the experts' advice,
But it didn't work (begging their pardon) –
All the birds have stayed well away,
Not a robin, a chaffinch or a jay.
Despite the nuts, crumbs, special seed,
The ornamental bird-bath, truth is that
My visitors to date have been
Eight pigeons, six sparrows – and next
door's cat!

FACELESS IN THE CROWD

Everybody who's who is here,
The Golf Club chairman and even a peer,
A rising pop group, our MP,
Two millionaires ... Do you see who I see? –
That actress from telly – and the Mayor!
It's such a sparkling, elegant affair,
All these well-known faces on show ...
I'm the only person here I don't know!

TIME, GENTLEMEN, PLEASE!

I know Rome wasn't built in a day,
But, please, my dear builder, may I say,
A kitchen extension, be it ever so pretty,
Should hardly take as long as the Eternal City!

I JUST DYED!

After being a dizzy blonde for years,
I went back to my own colour today,
What do you know, what a surprise,
I'm no longer a mouse – I'm grey!

STAIRWAY TO PARADISE

They say there's room at the top,
A saying you can't ignore:
I've just found a room to rent –
No lift – on the seventh floor!

NO LINGUA FRANCA

They say talk to your plants and they will
thrive,
Well, I've tried everything to keep mine
alive,
But they don't speak the same language as me,
For they're foreign – African violets, you see!

HANGOVER

The ''happy hour'' twixt six and seven
At my wine bar's really heaven,
All drinks half-price, isn't it swell
Except next day you feel like hell!

HAD MY CHIPS!

I'm redundant
Because of the new technology,
I've a microchip on my shoulder –
Can you blame me?

GOLD DIGGER

I told him I lived for the present,
And I thought he would understand:
I didn't mean living for today –
I meant a present in my hand!

INCOMPATIBLE

Although at first sight, he seemed meant
for me,
He had hang-ups galore,
He was into Zen, meditation, and
Vegetarian, what's more …
On the question of whether God exists,
All night he turned and tossed,
He said he was trying to find himself –
I told him to get lost!

BLONDES HAVE MORE FUN

My friend's 'phone hasn't stopped ringing,
She's much in demand everywhere,
Since she decided to go blonde,
She has all the fun of the fair!

OILING THE WHEELS

We decided to stop for a milk shake,
"What flavour?" my girl friend said.
"Banana, vanilla or chocolate …
Or shall we have oil sheiks instead!"

LOYAL FAN

I asked my son who'd won the match,
And all he said was, "Who cares?
Oh, all right, our team might have lost,
But our supporters beat theirs!"

ICING AGE

Of course she lies about her age,
If she told the truth, it would take
More candles to spell out her years
Than there's room on her birthday cake!

FAME-GAME

My friend is an actress,
So keen for fame,
Printed on her visiting cards
As well as her name,
Her telephone number,
And her address,
It says, "In case of accident,
Please ring up the Press"!

ALL WRAPPED UP

I know it's hot to be dressed like this,
Reason is:
My grannie says "Cast ne'er a clout,
Till May be out".
She has a *vested* interest in me!

EARLY BIRD

They call me the good-time girl,
But if you think that sounds great,
I'm not striking or swinging –
It's just that I'm never late!

EGO TRIP

I'm so helpful, I'm so sweet,
Witty, tender – and discreet ...
All these virtues without end –
Wish I had *me* as a friend!

TWICE UNBLESSED

I'm twice the woman I was,
A fact I do deplore,
For once I weighed seven stone two –
Now I'm fourteen stone four!

FACE VALUE

Beauty is only skin deep?
That's deep enough for me.
Who cares about the parts
That nobody's going to see!

BARE CHEEK!

I can't go away,
I've nothing to wear,
Do you want me to look like a tramp?
What's that you're saying?
I'll look simply great –
For we're going to a nudist camp!

INCLUDE ME OUT!

Go jogging? No, thank you,
I'd rather stay in bed.
Once went to a gym class –
Felt I'd been left for dead.
Swim? Aerobics? Squash? When
Tennis shoulder is rife?
Talk about exercise –
And I run for my life!

SAME OLD SOUVENIR

I've a souvenir of Blackpool,
Of course, the famous Tower,
And a cuckoo clock from Zurich
That cheeps on every hour.
Aphrodite's statue from Greece,
A straw donkey from Spain,
And a beer stein from Germany,
An ashtray from Bahrein,
Lace tablecloths from Portugal,
A French hand-painted fan …
They all have one thing in common –
They're all made in Taiwan!

LOAN SHARK

I've had a letter from the tax man,
He says I owe him a pretty penny,
But why is he demanding money –
I don't recall his lending me any!

FEATURING THE FAMILY

First, she lost pounds at a health farm,
Then she had her nose bobbed,
Said it was worth every penny,
Didn't feel she'd been robbed …
Cosmetic surgery? It's great,
She'd never hesitate.
So, should she be pleased or should she be mad? –
Everyone says she looks just like her dad!

SLIM CHANCE

I look great,
I look thin,
Long as I hold
My stomach in!

THANKS, I THINK!

I'm calling to thank you for the party,
I know it must have been great fun, my dear,
I mean when I feel this bad the next day,
Then I had a very good time, I fear!

NEW RHYMES FOR OLD

"Sing a song of sixpence,"
I started to recite.
"What's that?" queried my godchild,
"Are you sure you've got it right?"
Oh, what shall we do with the old rhymes
Now we're living in decimal times –
Sing a song of two and a half pee?
It doesn't have the same ring to me!

HAIRY PROBLEM

Why is it, whatever I do with my hair,
It never does turn out right?
When I became auburn overnight,
The man in my life took fright.
Then I went straight while the world
curled up;
Now I'm dark, to my sorrow,
For my new man's gazing at that blonde ...
I think I'll dye – tomorrow!

GOOD MUSE!

I don't need the poetry
Of Shakespeare, Yeats, Longfellow,
Tennyson, Keats or Wordsworth,
Be their verses oh, so mellow.
No, the words that touch my heart
When a garment I try on,
Are those two on the label
That simply say "Non Iron"!

FAIR PLAY

Mirror, mirror, on the wall,
Who is the fairest of them all?
Oh, please, don't answer right away,
I'm not looking my best today!

GOOD ADVICE

Early to bed and early to rise —
And you won't meet very swinging guys!

MODERN TIMES

She said she'd tell my fortune,
Read the future in my cup,
But I only had tea-bags,
So we gave the idea up!

SPOT THE DIFFERENCE

My hair looks great, my dress is new,
Tonight's the first date with you.
My eye shadow gleams – a subtle grey,
My lipstick matt – I'm on my way.
But will you tell me, please – if anyone knows …
Why's a spot appeared – on the end of my nose?

SHIPPING MAGNUM

We all know Helen was no plain Jane –
But a thousand ships launched – good gracious!
I think she did a deal in champagne –
On a "Sail or Return" basis!

IT'S A GIFT!

Nice girls get flowers,
But, methinks,
It's the minx
Who gets the minks!

MEMORIES ARE MADE OF THIS

Forgive and forget
That's what they say …
I forgive you, but
Forget? – No way!

SORRY, BUT ...

I don't think we'll be happy together,
For the problem is, truth to tell,
You say your wife doesn't understand you –
But I understand you too well!

ADVICE TO MEN

Want to succeed with women?
My advice, gentlemen, is sage:
Never forget her birthday –
And never remember her age!

BUSY LINE

This is not cousin Sue,
Or a shop that sells wine,
Or a radio phone-in,
Would you please clear the line!
It's not the rates office,
Or school for the rumba –
And I wish I knew where
You all get my number!

REAR VIEWS

I know what you say
About girls in pants,
There are those who can –
And those who can't!
But have you not seen
Yourself from the rear
And thought of wearing –
A kilt, my dear!

NEAT!

A stitch in time
Saves nine? –
For me, a pin's
Just fine!

COMPETITIVE SPIRIT

How I laughed when I beat you
At Scrabble, though you're a beginner …
I'm not just a bad loser –
I'm also a very bad winner!

THAT'S LIFE!

PEDIGREE PUP

We'd like an Alsatian
But the house is too small.
A chihuahua, a spaniel?
We ran through them all.

Maybe a corgi –
They've Royal approval –
A basset, a whippet,
A little black poodle?

Maybe a dachshund?
But look what we've got –
A sweet little puppy
Who's a bit of the lot!

REMEMBER ...?

Remember when we were very young –
Broad of mind and narrow of hip?
And now it's the other way around –
Getting older gives me the pip!

BEFORE AND AFTER

I'm waiting for my party guests,
Everything's been ready since five;
I said seven – it's seven now –
Will nobody ever arrive?

It's midnight and the flat's a mess,
Food all gone, ashtrays overflow,
Bill's drunk, the music's far too loud –
Oh, will nobody ever go!

ANIMAL MAGIC!

"Take four chicken legs," the recipe said,
And off to the supermarket I sped.
There were legs galore in packets of three,
As a student of zoology,
I find that a total mystery!

IT'S FRIENDSHIP!

My best friend came to tea today.
It was weeks since the last time we'd met.
There was so much gossip I hadn't heard –
Jean pregnant, Marcia in debt.

And Philippa Ann had run off last week
And left her three children behind.
Had I heard what Mary said about Dee –
And wasn't it awfully unkind?

My best friend admired my new deep freeze
And said how the baby had grown
My best friend said I looked terribly well –
Now I know I must lose half a stone!

KING REX

I tramp for miles and miles with you,
Beg the butcher for the juiciest bone,
Because I couldn't leave you behind,
Never go abroad, holiday at home …
It's a dog's life!

SOLO SONG

Life's very different since I got my divorce
(I was very happy to get it, of course).
But there are so many things to do or re-learn:
Mending a fuse, filling my income tax return.
Shall I still see his mother? Does the car need oil?
Where is the stop cock? Will carrots grow in this soil?
I must investigate strange noises in the night,
Zip up my own dress – rescue the dog from a fight …
And what do I do on Sundays now I'm a Miss,
For that's when I'm alone while the children are *his*.

COVER STORY

I disagree
With nudity.
It's disgusting,
Maladjusting.
Who wants to see
A naked he,
Or she, indeed …
So please take heed:
Let modesty
Your watchword be,
And on the beach
I do beseech,
Keep up the tone –
At least till I've lost
half a stone!

DEADLY SILENT

My dog is very quiet,
But he thinks it such a lark
To terrorise the postman –
His bite is worse than his bark!

LIBERATED LADIES

Equal pay,
Labours shared,
Free contraception,
Bosoms bared.
Families planned,
Abortion on demand,
Maternity leave –
We know where we stand
We sit and talk of women's rights –
And dream of men and love-warmed nights.

STOUT PARTY

Friends for a party,
The fare must be hearty.
I'll bake sausage rolls
And there'll be bowls
Of savoury dips
And wafer thin chips,
Canapés galore,
Cheese, cake, petits fours …

My friends take the drink,
From the food they shrink …

When I give a do, tell me why it
Happens everyone's on a diet?

ADVICE CENTRE

Without our weekly sessions,
I don't know what I'd do,
Discussing all my problems
And thinking them right through.
He's wise and sympathetic
And always understands,
Confidentially, I'd say
I'm in the best of hands.
So till the next appointment
(And thanks for your advice),
Oh, incidentally …
This hair-style's really nice!

PASSING STRANGERS

I hadn't seen him for fifteen years,
The man I once wanted to be mine,
His hair had thinned, his waist had thickened,
To think I once found him divine!
I was pleased time had treated me well,
And I knew that I looked just the same,
Then our hostess introduced us and
He said: "Sorry, didn't catch your name"!

GREAT NIGHT OUT

Didn't you think Joyce was looking old?
And those canapés she served were absolutely cold.
Oh, what did you think of Ben's new wife?
Well, I tell you quite frankly, I wouldn't have
her life
After what Jean told me about *him*.
Wasn't their new drawing-room furniture simply
grim?
Joe there alone; said Sue was away –
You can see there are problems with that marriage,
I'd say.
Ann's children are ill-behaved, aren't they?
And Sam's still drinking – did you see what
he put away?
That dress of Lynn's – wasn't it tarty?
Must write to say thank you. Wasn't it a great
party!

CHORE BORE

They say it's a man's world,
Don't believe what they say,
I'd hate to be a man
And have to shave each day.

PUPPY LOVE

Take the puppy for a walk,
Teach him to sit up and beg,
Find for him a friendly tree,
Stop him nipping postman's leg.

Give him food three times a day,
Enrol him in obedience school –
Get from him a doleful look –
How can I be so awfully cruel?

Hubby home to barks of glee
As I clean up another mess,
Puppy licks him, wags his tail –
Dog is *man's* best friend – yes!

MARRIAGE LINES

Something old,
Something new,
Something borrowed,
Something blue …
I'm old,
You're new;
You borrowed my husband –
I'm blue.

THE GRAPEVINE

Robert got drunk at the vicar's party,
The new folk at no. 9 are the Flynns,
Mrs Hope had tea with Russell Harty,
And she's heard that Jane is expecting twins.
The milkman's running in a marathon,
The Bennetts had burglars – such a pity,
Don't wait for the post – it's been and gone,
The Jones are moving – tired of the city.
If you find her cat, please tell Miss Faber,
The Priors are parting – such a sensation,
When you have such a well-informed neighbour,
There's no need for a local news station!

ALL FOR LOVE

You say you can't do enough for me,
My commands, you say, are your wishes ...
Well, how can I answer, but to ask –
Forget it. Just help with the dishes!

FRIDAY THE THIRTEENTH

The alarm didn't ring
So I missed my train,
Then I laddered my tights,
Got caught in the rain.
Now I sit by the 'phone
But still you've not rung –
Oh, yes, it's one of those days
When the policemen look young!

ADOPTION

You didn't give birth to him,
He was born to another,
But you've loved and cherished him –
So you are his real mother.

OPEN TICKET

I've travelled the world twice over,
Met the famous: saints and sinners,
Poets and artists, kings and queens,
Old stars and hopeful beginners.
I've been where no one's been before,
Learned secrets from writers and cooks –
All with one library ticket
To the wonderful world of books.

DOG'S LIFE

Not again, I groan, mopping up the mess ...
Now you can't teach an old dog new tricks
we're told,
But looking at my pup and the puddle
He's made – I wish I could teach new ones the old!

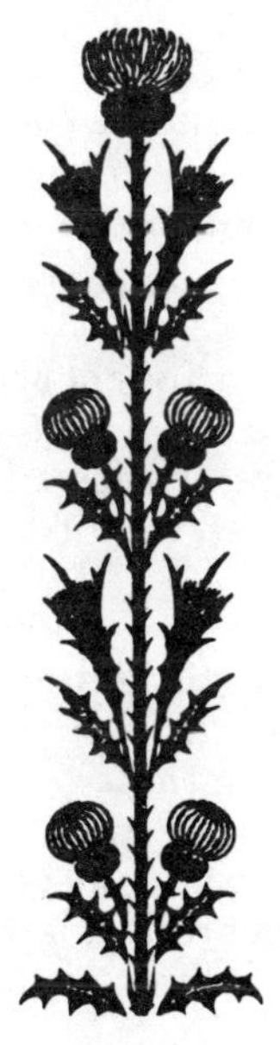

WHEN WE WERE YOUNG

I think of all the fun we had
And how your eyes are blue
And when I remember Venice,
It's just in terms of you.

With aching heart, I remember
That sun-drenched week in Spain,
The very first time you kissed me …
Didn't it ever rain?

Were we really always singing,
The world ours on a plate?
Why is it though I want to go,
I forget the rows and hate

And the way we fought about money
And hurt each other's pride,
And tried to break each other's heart –
We tried, oh yes, we tried.

For so long now, we've known it's wrong
And yet we've still gone on –
Is it because of the good times –
Or fear of being alone

I know we've got to say goodbye
And make the break at last,
For we've no future together –
Only past.

INTERIOR MONOLOGUE

I've had my wrinkles smoothed away,
Breasts lifted, buttocks flattened,
My nose owes more to art than life,
My figure I have patterned.

I'm into Zen and oestrogen too,
Read all the latest books.
Alcohol? – Oh, not for me,
I'm noted for my looks.

See me in a good light,
You'd never guess my age.
I visit this marvellous doctor
Who's becoming all the rage.

By trendy gossip columnists,
My praises they are sung.
But if I look so blooming marvellous,
Tell me – why don't I *feel* young?

POLITICS OF ENVY

I've skimped and scraped and paid my dues,
Decided I can't afford new shoes,
Eat fish and eggs – steaks now are dreams,
Re-cover chairs, let out more seams.
Yet still I see women swathed in minks,
Buying expensive food and drinks,
And it seems to me so unjust –
That the rich are always with us.

ROLES

A woman is a sometime thing.
Sometimes a mother, sometimes a wife,
Sometimes a sister, a nurse with your life
In her hands.
Sometimes a lover, sometimes a worker,
Often a listener, occasionally a shirker.
Sometimes this and sometimes that –
(Usually the lady who feeds the cat)
A gossip, a poet, a cook … Declaim it:
She's whatever is needed. You name it.
And sometimes I think, with this
incredible range –
Wouldn't it be nice to be *me* for a change.

DEDICATED

You know those dedications
In the front of books,
Like, "For Mother who helped",
Or "To All Britain's Dukes"?
And "For Susan" or (cryptic)
"With love to G.T."?
Well, when I write a book
That won't be for me.
I won't say "For Simon",
Nor yet "For Honey",
I'll simply acknowledge
I wrote it "For Money".

DOWN UNDER

You say it's tough at the top,
I'm sure you're being sincere,
But you should be at the bottom –
And see what the view's like from here!

NICE TO BE NEEDED

I thought no one cared I was alive,
That was a depressing thought to me,
But then the tax man sent me a bill,
And the gas and electricity …
So people *do* care that I'm alive –
I'm vital to the economy!

TAKE BACK YOUR PEARLS

"The world's your oyster,
Just waiting," said he.
Pity that oysters
Disagree with me!

SLIM CHANCES

I've dieted and exercised,
At last I've got back into shape,
I'm no longer shunning the scales,
Or even afraid of the tape
Measure!
Pleasure …
To wear a bikini again,
Ask if they have it in size ten!
But sad to relate, though I *want* to
stay thinner,
Every man I meet now invites me to dinner!

CLOCKING OUT

A present should suit the recipient
But donors aren't always percipient:
My aunt was always late for work
For she never cared about time,
Yet when she retired they gave her
A clock with a very nice chime!

SINISTER STREET

It's sad how times have changed
And impressions do not tally,
What I called "Lovers' Lane"
My children call "Muggers' Alley"!

MY WAY

What will people say?
If it weren't for that thought,
So many people
Would live life as they ought.

SETBACK

Keep right on to the end of the road,
Don't shilly-shally, don't look back;
Good advice but when I took it
My road turned out a cul-de-sac!

HOBSON'S CHOICE

Tinker, tailor, soldier, spy,
What profession shall have I?
Once we could rejoice
That we had the choice …
Now
Kids are overjoyed
If they're just employed.

SKIN DEEP

Oh, how can you purr
At the sight of fur?
Mink?
Think!
Of animal farms —
Don't they give you qualms?

And extinct is forever,
So it's not very clever
To wear a leopard coat that's real,
(Sealskin looks better on a seal).

They say beauty is just skin deep,
But if you wear real furs,
It's not even as deep as that,
For the skin isn't yours!

IT'S TOUGH AT THE TOP

You've got money,
And you've got looks,
You're sought after,
You've written books ...
You're not happy,
Reason, I guess,
You're a failure
As a success.

PROGRESS?

It was safe to walk home alone at night,
People knew their place – and wrong from right,
You got what you paid for, come what might ...
Things aren't what they used to be.

We don't send children up chimneys anymore,
We don't turn pregnant girls from the door,
You can see a doctor though you're poor ...
Things aren't what they used to be.

Why do we throw the good out with the bad?
A thought we should all find very sad.
Let's think about things.

REVERSE

The council had a brilliant idea,
They gave poets' names to the new estates,
Calling them Keats, Shelley, Wordsworth
and Donne,
Byron, Shakespeare, Milton, Browning
and Yeats ...
Just look at them. Architecturally,
They wouldn't rate one line of poetry.

NOT RESTING ON MY LAURELS

I went to the Queen's garden party,
Smiled at Prince Charles as he went by,
Wrote a poem about the Queen Mother,
Queued for hours for a glimpse of Di,
Rhapsodised about the Royal christening
But I guess no one was listening,
For, alas, alack, I do regret,
I was not made Poet Laureate!